PAINFUL PASSAGE, JOYFUL JOURNEY

PAINFUL PASSAGE, JOYFUL JOURNEY

A memoir, the story of God and me

SUSAN A. COOPER

RESOURCE *Publications* · Eugene, Oregon

PAINFUL PASSAGE, JOYFUL JOURNEY
A memoir, the story of God and me

Resource Publications
An Imprint of Wipf and Stock Publishers
199 W. 8th Ave., Suite 3
Eugene, OR 97401

www.wipfandstock.com

PAPERBACK ISBN: 979-8-3852-0470-0
HARDCOVER ISBN: 979-8-3852-0471-7
EBOOK ISBN: 979-8-3852-0472-4

01/04/24

Painful Passage, Joyful Journey is dedicated to God, my heavenly Father, to Jesus, my Savior and to the Holy Spirit, my comforter and guide. It is also devoted to my dearest friend, my daily reminder of God's intimate love, my husband of fifty-five years, Ivan Cooper.

"For I know the plans I have for you," declares the Lord, "plans to prosper you and not to harm you, plans to give you hope and a future."

—Jer 29:11 NIV

Contents

CONTENTS

PREFACE

FRAGILITY

A glass ornament hanging precariously
I had been thrust from the branch
The shattered pieces miniscule
Unfixable. . .until God gathered the shards.

My story is a patchwork tapestry with loose threads; the journey is not linear, but life seldom is.

This saga weaves through years of deep valleys and occasional moments of euphoria. The purpose of committing this voyage is to share the life lessons that I too frequently accepted belatedly or resentfully.

The integral theme throughout these seventy plus years has been the unrelenting pursuit that God launched on my behalf. During the darkest junctures, He persisted. God's hand was on me in the form of Abba, a loving Father to an orphan, as Jesus my Savior, Friend, Healer, and through the Holy Spirit, guiding and directing. Often God's intimate care has been demonstrated through the kindness, compassion and support of others. ("Be not forgetful to entertain strangers: for thereby some have entertained angels unawares" Hebrew 13:2, KJV.)

There are reoccurring themes of betrayal, abandonment, fear, loneliness, and of love, faith, hope and healing. God at the center demonstrates how an extraordinary heavenly Father can transform the life of a tragic figure. This is the story I want to share because it points to the fact that if we accept His invitation He will rewrite our lives. I am proof. . .

The story of God and me is the tale of a spiritual journey, a quest for a loving Father, and too often, my attempt to be "god." It has no real beginning point, for my saga did not begin with my birth, the tragedies of a lost childhood, my marriage, or even the conscious examination that led to this chronicles. This odyssey has been raw, painful and surprisingly blessed.

Harnessing the events so that others too may experience the intimacy of God's hand is the task with which I grapple. The map to this point has frequently been unchartered and permeated with physical and psychological detours. This story will weave in and out of childhood because my life has. Paraphrasing Dickens, perhaps I should begin with "the best of times" adulthood. Although it has not idyllic, and frequently has been fraught with real-life struggles, if there had been no Ivan, there would be no narrative, for there would be no me. To get to Ivan some chronology is necessary. . .so perhaps "the worst of times" should set the stage.

Most of us exist in realities that are dichotomous: good or bad. The first six years of my life were, by recollection, extraordinarily safe, loving and hopeful. I waltzed through those years securely happy. There was a rhythm that included by big brother's Catholic education, my days of ransacking his toy box, our mother's hours in her art studio or resting, and always, the nightly read aloud sessions shared with our parents. We thumbed our way through the unabridged classics as I learned to read. Few vignettes emerge that do not merge into the landscape of a happy home.

And so, in seeking a beginning to this tale of God and me, I wonder whether early tragedy ushers us more quickly into the arms of God.

Richard Rohr (*Falling Upward*, 2011) wrote about the sacred wounds that both liberate self and others. God used the traumas that spanned childhood, adolescence and my young adult years to liberate me. Once free, the story became a *Psalm of Praise.*

ACKNOWLEDGMENTS

The list of those who have prayed, read, listened and shared the process of bringing this memoir to fruition is voluminous. Fearful of oversight, I am going to recognize that this endeavor was encouraged by family, friends, colleagues and students, all of whom played a vital role. The task was prayerfully launched and guided by the Holy Spirit as I sought to pen a *Psalm of Praise*.

INTRODUCTION

The narrative of my personal experiences are viewed through multiple lens: the six year old child so violently wretched from a loving family by the murder/suicide of her parents, the little girl who lost her big brother as they physically and emotionally separated for life, the decade of abuse in the home of a relative, the wounded adult confronting the past in order to have a future, the healed survivor re-examining six plus decades of lies and betrayals, and in the midst of it all, the constant presence of a loving God.

This is my perception, and thus my story, as I attempt to reconstruct a painful past, permeated by the presence of an intimate loving Father. It is God's persistence in orchestrating an ordinary child into a person of faith that is the core of this journey. The events of my life may be reconstructed by others through their outside lens, but it is my truth, my saga.

BOOK ONE

.

THE CHARADE

THE SETTING

A cozy brick cottage
A wood burning fireplace
Dormers with freshly starched country curtains
Smells of paint and turpentine
Of wood fires and fresh flowers
A clipped lawn with large trees
Sidewalks
A church across the street
Godparents next door
Could it happen here?
Murder/suicide.

A beautiful, artistic mother, a loving Irish Catholic father, a cerebral big brother, and a precocious princess created a Norman Rockwell picture of stability, of love, faith, and safety. That portrait was shattered four days after the celebration of my sixth birthday.

The party was documented with Brownie Box cameras, and by all evidence, it was a success. The neighboring children were decked out in their Sunday clothes. There were games, refreshments, and prizes. Packages were unwrapped, and leftover birthday cake was stored in the refrigerator. In less than a week, the devoted husband and doting father killed his pretty wife, and then turned the gun on himself.

Decades later, I would awaken at 3:23 a.m. trying to breath, attempting to make sense of the panic attack that left me so horribly frightened, unable to return to sleep. At six, I did not remember hearing gun shots in the night, I only knew that my brother and I were hungry, and there were no sounds from the kitchen. We tried to open their bedroom door, but it was locked. Tommy hoisted me through an unlocked window, and I found death.

There are vague memories of walking across the street to our Godparents' home, of police sirens, and relatives arriving. Tommy and I were restricted from the funeral. We were told to select a single item to take with us as the relatives formed a caravan from Kentucky to Texas. I chose the vanity table my mother had constructed for my Christmas, but was told that it was too large to transport. The shiny red tricycle I rode around and around the block waiting for Tommy to emerge from the school bus was then selected.

We headed south, gripping hands in the back seat of one of the cars. Little of that trip remains in my mind, but the arrival in Houston is dramatically and forever etched in my memory. The caravan parked in front of one of the relative's houses, and five sets of aunts and uncles surrounded the car in which Tommy and I were seated. The dialogue began with questions of who could take one of us, and responses of why it was not feasible. Within an hour, I lost my big brother to an aunt who did not want him, and I was handed over to another and her seventh husband. Fear was the overwhelming emotion then, and for the following decade.

MEMORIES OF A CHILDHOOD LOST

1948–1954

Six years erased
There must have been Christmas in that Irish Catholic home
Were there trees, stockings, carols, cookies. . .
Fleeting glimpses of moments of happiness
Sand crabs on a beach
The Chicago zoo
A cough and a teaspoon of honey brought by a mother
Books read aloud before bedtime
Voyages into the lives of Peter Pan and Oliver Twist
Sparse recollections of another time, of safety and freedom from fear
Gunshots eradicated my childhood.

I loved my father with the pure love of a six year old daughter who knows her importance in his world. I was his cherished princess, adored and virtually faultless.

The earliest memory I hold is of my father teaching me to wink. The front seat of the 1953 Studebaker was the classroom, and the classes were held at traffic lights and stop signs. The tests were passed when passers-by could be distracted. Laughter and a father's pride in "his Irish princess" were a part of those lessons.

Baptism in the Catholic chapel was a day of importance. The nuns in their long black habits were frightening, but my daddy was so pleased that his beloved wife and two children joined his chosen church. He taught me that God loved me, and that I could talk to Him anytime I wanted. This foundational understanding of a heavenly Father who would never abandon me was core to the years that followed.

Then the center of my universe abandoned me in a pool of crimson, and took the beautiful lady who brought me honey when I coughed, who was his wife, and the mother about which I have so few recollections.

My mother did not name me, she asked her oldest sister to suggest a name. Tommy, my big brother, was named after a famous Irish patriot, and our father. The woman who read insatiably, was an artist, could not or would not select a name for her only daughter. It is no wonder that I have few memories of her.

The world in which I lived for those six years was encapsulated; it primarily consisted of two parents, and a big brother. Tommy was my hero, he could read, and he was smart. The adoration I had for him was not reciprocated. He had been their sole focus for five years, and he deeply resented my arrival. Oblivious to his distain, I followed him everywhere, and tried to emulate all he did well.

Sixty-nine years after the event, there are facial scars that speak to my big brother's distain of an added sibling. Tommy was given a bb gun and a careful tutorial to never point it toward any living being. Our father did not reach the house before Tommy turned the gun on me and shot twice. The gun was confiscated, and my brother did not sit comfortably for awhile. It did not end the resentment, however.

There were times when he was kind, and caring. Tommy held my hand as we boarded the bus to the Owensboro theatre. *Peter Pan* was screening, and our parents had just read the unabridged version aloud. That was a magical day.

Tommy got carsick, or so he said
Tommy got to ride up front in the brand new Studebaker
My announcements that I was sick, too, were unheeded
My complaints that it was too hot were ignored
Whining did not help
Announcing that the suitcase was scrunching me wasn't noted
So opening the case, and watching the brightly colored garments tumble down the
Texas road was joyfully entertaining, until I got caught.

There was Laddie, a large collie, who was mostly Tommy's dog and companion. He was left behind when we were taken by the relatives. No one has ever explained. . .It is no wonder that Tommy is so afraid of attachments.

BIG BROTHER

Childhood memories arise with the mention of my big brother
He was smart and very old
His toy chest was abandoned for the books he loved
The Erector Set and the red wagon became mine
His football stayed hidden lest our father suggest a game of toss
His bicycle demanded too much coordination, and too much time away from his books
A disappointed father, a proud mother loved that big brother
But it was his little sister who saw him as a hero
He read to her
Held her hand on the bus
Took her to see Peter Pan

Promised to always take care of her. . .

Where did that brother go?

Did the same gun that took the lives of our parents destroy the eleven year old forever?

Sixty-nine years he has been lost to me, and to himself

STOLEN MEMORIES

Too often the gaps of those early years were filled in with the perceptions of others: "Aunt Mildy" and "Uncle Joe," best friends to our parents, Grandma Davis, the loving mother of my mom, my angry, damaged brother and the aunt with whom I spent the next ten years. . .the versions were diverse, and did little to provide a framework for a childhood that was destroyed by acts of violence. The stories, as told to me, did not resonate as a part of my history, but they were repeated so frequently that I began to assume that there was something true in the vignettes about a courageous, tenacious, confident child who explored her world with abandonment. I was no longer that child. . .

Did I really get run over crossing a boulevard in Oklahoma City? Scraped up by the under carriage of the automobile, but saved from physical and emotional distress?

Was I the child who at the age of three abandoned my clothes to wander up the hill to visit the beekeeper and his wife? The story was that I was reclaimed as the wardrobe path led my distraught parents to their "lost" daughter.

Clothes seemed to be an early fascination. There were tales of a family holiday during which I was left unattended in the backseat of the Studebaker while my parents crooned over a carsick brother. Miles later a check on the small daughter in the back revealed a suitcase open and empty. Wardrobe items had drifted colorfully in the winds for miles.

The beautiful mother took frequent naps, and although the hook to the door had been relocated to thwart my escape, I apparently learned to maneuver the counter and unlatch the door to freedom. Snatching the forbidden wagon (it was Tommy's), I ran the sidewalks beyond our house. Reputedly I rescued a small boy from a mean mother, and took him home in the wagon. The result was a long search for his family, and embarrassing enquiries as to whether anyone was missing a child.

There was the glorious sixth birthday party, attended by my beloved maternal grandmother, my favorite uncle, Don, lots of laughing children, and me. I have only a memory of birthday cake in the refrigerator the morning that Tommy and I woke up hungry, the morning that our childhoods ended.

Sixty-nine years later, there are no answers. The brother who could illuminate the world in which we lived is still unable to face it. There are police reports and newspaper clippings, and little else upon which to build a foundation for a life that was plunged into the abyss for more than a decade.

LIFE REDEFINED

Upon arrival, Tommy and I were separated, and separated we have been throughout the ensuing years. Physically we were "dished out" to unwilling aunts and uncles, our mother's siblings, geographically isolating us from the only remaining family we had: one another. Neither of us were wanted by the relatives, but denied a haven with the family friends who begged for us to be together and with them. The underlining issue was "what would people think." A fabricated story was developed to explain the death of the beloved sister and her husband. It was framed as an automobile accident, and the benevolent care takers as self sacrificing.

Tommy was wrenched away from the sister he had promised to always protect, and I was taken to the aunt's house to meet her seventh husband and her daughter, six months my senior. Terrified without Tommy at my side, I climbed out of the backseat of the car. Within minutes my sole possession, the shiny red tricycle, was given to the aunt's daughter, and I was delegated the owner of her old, much smaller bike. It was a defining moment that predicted the ambiance of the next decade.

Day one ushered in an era of turmoil, fear, abuse, and lies. *The Rules* were clearly delineated: I was forbidden to talk about my parents to anyone. Questions about their deaths would be handled by the aunt. If I breached the stipulation, I would be severely punished. This proved to be true. When asked by a caring first grade teacher, I talked of the blood, the gun, the loss. That prompted a call to the aunt, who clothed the revelation in lies. She defined me as an ungrateful child with an active imagination. The contrived story was then repeated. My confinement to a locked room followed the telephone conversion.

The Rule that dominated the decade in Texas was to keep the myth of my parents' deaths unspoken. There were, however, rules for almost everything. At the time of awakening a bathroom trip was mandated; hair and teeth were brushed and hands washed, or there was no breakfast, and no second chances. Table manners were integral to each meal; a request for food without a "please and thank you" resulted in immediate dismissal from the table and no more food for the remainder to the day. All offered menu items were to be eaten, with mouth closed while chewing. Refusal to finish a portion meant confinement at the table until I complied. It is important to note that these rules did not apply to the aunt, the uncle, or the cousin. On one glorious occasion I managed to slip slimy okra into the flower vase; Victory!

The nightmares and bedwetting began immediately, as did the punishments for waking up the aunt and soiling her bed linens. The humiliation at her constant recital of the ways I was unappreciative for all she was doing for me was ongoing. The neighbors, relatives, and church congregation soon applauded her kindness in taking in an ungrateful, difficult orphan.

It was on that foundation that her daughter established a rationale for bullying me throughout the years. I had disrupted her childhood, her mother resented my existence, so she had license to threaten, hurt, and frighten me with the full knowledge that if her behavior was revealed, I would be the punished one. This scenario was the fabric of my day-to-day existence.

The house in which we lived was physically lovely, and for a short time I was given a room to myself. It was in that room that God's presence became so evident. At night, alone and so afraid, I would talk to Him. He heard my woeful cries, my loneliness, confusion and permeating fear. There was a calming sense of no longer being alone, an assurance that I was loved, and guarded. Through the years I came to learn that I did not have to talk to Him on my knees (after many sleepless nights beside that built-in bed), and that He was with me through the daylight hours as well.

A kindergarten dropout, I did not return to school until the fall of 1954. It was there that I learned that there were ways to vicariously escape the aunt, the fear, the abuse. . .Books became the vehicle that propelled me through the long Texas years.

LIFELINES

First grade was an escape. There were books, lots of books, and I had been a reader before my parents' deaths. There were friends, and there was kindness. I soared because I was in an environment that was a haven. Arithmetic was the sole academic challenge, but the rest of each school day was a getaway. Too soon the school bus heralded me back to the place of fear.

Quite literally God used literature to remove me from the cycle of fear. It was through the pages of stories that I learned to hope, and to hold to the promise that someday I would again find a world where safety and love existed. At night, consumed by fear, I escaped from the aunt, the cousin, the dispassionate uncle, and became Heidi with the Alms Uncle, herding goats with Peter, and reveling in the serenity of the mountains. *Heidi* (Spyri,1881)was sent by the family friends, "Aunt" Mildy and "Uncle" Joe the first Christmas I was with the aunt. I slept with the treasured book under my pillow for years.

The aunt was a voracious reader with an extensive library and I had free license to take books off the shelves. It was a collection of classic literature that became as vital to my survival as my friendship with God. When and how much I read soon became a topic of constant contention, however.

I soon made two literary discoveries that propped me up for years. I met the Marsh family through the pages of *Little Women* (Alcott,1868) and became inspired by Jo to record my own stories. It was the death of Beth that caught my tightly held grief off guard, and facilitated the mourning process of parents gone and life re-written. The horror that had been so shut away was penetrated by Louisa May Alcott's story, and allowed me to cry for the Marsh family, and for all that I had lost.

It was the discovery of Charles Dickens' compassion for orphans that emboldened my dreams of freedom one day. Oliver Twist (Dickens,1838) escaped the Children's Home and Fagin to find a safe haven, and I would too, one day. . .David Copperfield's (Dickens, 1850) wicked step-father elicited my hatred, and served as a proxy for the aunt. At the age of eight, it was in the pages of my beloved books that I found solace and friends; I lived the stories I read and became Jo Marsh, the aspiring author, David meeting Mr. Micawber, Laura Engle Wilder at Plum Creek and the Big Woods (Wilder, 1937 and 1932), Colin in a "secret garden" (Burnett, 1911). . .each new title was an adventure that left me changed, enriched, better. I learned to experience through others' lens what I was forbidden to acknowledge myself; I grieved and cried, and clutched God's hand.

A pattern developed that provided an additional respite. My maternal grandmother arrived late each fall and stayed through the New Year. The aunt's abuse was less overt with the presence of her mother, and I breathed a bit more freely. Even during those annual visits there were times of cruelty. During one such visit I developed a severe chest cold. It was frigid by Texas standards, but we traveled to a nearby coastal resort for seafood. The restaurant was posh and crowded. Repeatedly I politely excused myself from the dining table to blow my nose in the Ladies' Room. After my third or fourth departure, I was told that I was disrupting everyone's good time, and I was sent, without dinner, to wait in the cold car. I remember being hurt, very cold, hungry and frightened. Even my loving grandmother stayed in the restaurant enjoying holiday fare while her small granddaughter waited alone in the frigid car.

Second grade offered a different kind of rescue; I contracted the German Measles! For two weeks I was in quarantine. The aunt left food on a tray outside the door, and all contact with the family was forbidden. I recall it as my happiest time during those ten years. My room was full of books, and the aunt and cousin were "at bay."

It was also in my second year of school that teachers began to note that I was an accelerated reader/writer, and an engaged student. I was selected to "star" in the school Christmas pageant. Although there was resentment over the attention I was receiving, especially since the cousin was not selected to participate, I was allowed to contribute.

The summer between my second and third year of elementary school an additional trauma occurred: the aunt kicked husband number seven out of "her" bedroom, and he was delegated to my room. That introduced a new terror; I was forced to share a bedroom with the cousin.

THE COUSIN

For two and a half years the cousin had been a rival. My arrival had diminished her status as the only child, pampered and indulged. The year age difference placed her in school at the time of my arrival. The focus of her life shifted dramatically, and the primary goal seemed always to make mine as miserable as possible.

Due to the cousin's slightly bigger stature and strength, I was an easy target for daily punches. A favorite practice was to push me to the ground (frequently with the assistance of her best friend, a neighbor and a bully), sit on my stomach and hold Spanish Moss over my mouth and nose. Reporting such events only resulted in punishment for me, because among the rules in that family, and there were many, NO TATTLING was key, but only if I was the one relating grievances.

Until the room shift I had been able to escape into a place where God waited every evening, and where I could pray and read without disturbance. Sharing a room with the cousin added a level of personal peril that I had not previously experienced. It began quite simply with her declaration that I should not sleep because she would kill me during the night. . . This "promise" continued through her pre-adolescent years, at which time her shift moved toward boys.

There was a direct correlation between the cousin's hatred of me and her mother's abuse. My invasion of the cousin's space heightened the bullying and the aunt's need to prove that her daughter was still the center of her universe. Most of the mistreatment was psychological with constant declarations of how like my father I was, and how unlike my beautiful, artistic mother. Punishment for nightmares from which I awoke screaming, tightly harnessed the rule that there would be no discussion of my parents, death, fear. . .ended in physical abuse beyond the cousin's pummeling. The aunt used willow switches freely, but more often she employed flagrant lies.

There were promises: if you don't cry when the dentist extracts your molars, you can go to the movie. . .followed by a caveat of interpretation. I was not brave enough, therefore the promise was null. You may take dance lessons, but the cousin did not, therefore you may not. Piano lessons were a carrot until the cousin reminded all that she did not have musical lessons. Inconsistency was rampant, and the unpredictable made day-to-day life dangerous. It was a quicksand existence where a single word from the cousin could reverse everything previously negotiated.

The neighbor's dog scaled the chain linked fence and attacked the aunt's cat; it was, of course, my fault. A firecracker exploded in the aunt's hand, and I had somehow caused it. The ungrateful, lazy niece who was such a burden became more of a problem as time passed.

During the third year in Texas, the cousin and I formed an alliance over a frightening scenario. It took weeks for us to rally the courage to talk to the aunt about a situation that victimized both of us. It was common ground, and for a moment we were "friends."

An older step-brother lived nearby with his wife and two young daughters. The aunt visited him frequently, although I have no recollection of him at the aunt's house, ever. The cousin and I would be required to go along on these visits, and were regularly sent to take a nap while the adults talked. The adult father of two female children began to check on us, and to inappropriately touch us. At first we both pretended to be asleep, too frightened to react. With this shared experience of horror, we told the aunt of the abuse. She promised to "talk to her son," and she continued to take us on the forced visits. The issue was as muted as the truth of my parents' deaths.

The bond with the cousin quickly evaporated as her mother's promise to intervene was nulled. So tragic. . .

FEAR

THE MONSTER WITHIN

There was a darkness within so terrifying that I could not admit it
To myself, to God
Identifying it might empower the monster
Would my Heavenly Father abandon me if I told Him of the
darkness?
A father's legacy: violence
The hatred I had for the aunt, the cousin, the parents who deserted
Strangled with fear of blood, loud noises, anger, guns, myself. . .
Could I become my father?

The confusion became more intense as the precarious tightrope of
life kept me forever on guard. The aunt was a "pillar" at the Presbyterian Church where she was lauded for her kindness toward
the troubled, belligerent orphan taken into her home. The façade
was difficult as the aunt delineated the long list of infractions I had
logged the previous week.

Deep inside my mind I knew that my parents did not die in an
automobile accident, and I experienced shame and guilt wonder-
ing if I had somehow caused their deaths. There was little contact
with my brother, just rare annual visits with no time to talk, even if

he had been willing to do so. I became afraid beyond the ongoing fear of the aunt's anger. Death loomed, and so during that dark period, I began what has become the most intimate relationship of my life; I turned to a Heavenly Father and cried for my parents, for my lost childhood, for my brother, and I talked to Him about the permeating terror with which I lived.

It was at this point that I believe God began the long journey of using my wounds to heal me.

A LITTLE INDEPENDENCE

The fall of 1960 was significant. I was free of the cousin for entire days; the school bus stopped at the junior high building before reaching my site of sanction, the elementary school. I was without constant scrutiny and tattling that year. It proved to be a period of consequence for a number of reasons.

The new sixth grade teacher warned us daily of impending attacks from the Communist. Forced to crawl under the desks and protect our necks with clasped hands was a routine activity. So, I added another fear to my voluminous list: an unknown enemy wanted to kill me.

A stellar student, I had learned to read all required textbooks early in the school year so that I could hide my cherished "real books" between the pages of science, history, math. . .and escape the no longer stimulating academic routines. It was during this fateful year that I was caught reading Laura Ingalls Wilder during geography. The trip to the office resulted in my aunt's appearance. As she berated my laziness and ingratitude, the principal calmly focused on my intellect and my need to be challenged. It was an affirmation I sorely needed.

It was also a time of awkwardness. . .

Reflections are amazing ways of seeing God at work in our lives. The years leading up to adolescence were raw and painful. The cousin was stunningly beautiful, and I was an awkward, ungainly mess. There were metal braces on my teeth, enhanced by rubber bands that held the top and bottom teeth in alignment. Corrective shoes weighing more than my legs adorned my feet. The bright orange hair that had been charming when I was a young girl, was frizzy, unruly and vibrant. At five feet five inches tall, my seventy-three pounds were pitifully distributed. I loved school and books, was homely and cognizant of that fact, and shared a room with a boy-crazed cousin.

In retrospect I realize that I was also desperately in need of love, acceptance and a feeling of worth. A bookworm with a chest so flat that it was introverted, I received no attention from males at church or school. It was painful to look in the mirror, and more so at the cousin who was lauded by her mother and every guy with whom she interacted. It took years for me to recognize that my social awkwardness was a blessing in disguise. God was protecting me from decisions that may have fleetingly provided a balm, and then would have left scars of shame and guilt.

The clumsy years were also times of astonishing disclosures. The summer of 1961, I was thirteen. After a brief visit with my maternal grandmother, I was invited to stay with "Aunt Mildy" and "Uncle Joe," the family friends that had given up on trying to pry me away from the Texas relatives. My big brother, Tommy, had joined them the previous year as a permanent member of the household. So I was reunited with my brother and the children of the family friends for a brief summer. There were four of us, the oldest just out of high school, my big brother entering his senior year, a daughter two and a half years older than me, and of course, me.

It was during this visit that I began to talk about the death of my parents. Tommy would not, or could not, address the questions, but Lea allowed me to talk, and she responded. I was told that they were told not to talk of the murder/suicide because the aunt had forbidden any reference. The general idea was that I was so young at the time, I probably did not remember. . .

The guilt, fear and confusion that I had held in the deepest recesses of my mind for seven long years poured forth in tears, and then in a consuming anger for all of those who had denied me the truth: my big brother, the family friends, my maternal grandmother, and most specifically the aunt. Hatred reared. . .

TEXAS

THE UNCLE. . .

Russell smoked cigars
Boxed aboard a naval battleship during WWII
Came from the country
Was evangelical
Cherished his Model A truck
Offered rides to military hitchhikers
Cooked hamburger casseroles
Taught me to ride a bike
Fought with the aunt
Facilitated my escape
Killed himself.

At six, I knew the uncle was also unhappy. He was husband number seven, successful, but he was not one of the early millionaires she had snagged. They had no common ground. She read Dickens, he boxed. The daughter was the sole connector. His people were Texas dirt farmers raising watermelons and peanuts in the Panhandle, hers were educators. Church was a proper pretense for her, faith was fundamental to him.

One Christmas the cousin and I were awakened by the sound of sleigh bells. We were herded to the window to witness Santa himself in the backyard. He waved, and we were hurried back into bed with the admonishment that Santa would not come inside unless we were asleep. That was a moment of wonder, long before I realized that it was a gift from the uncle.

Through the years there were memories of his stances against the aunt on my behalf. They were sparse, and I came to understand that he too, was afraid. A simple man, a Navy boxer, he reached out in loneliness and married a shrew. My life was tragic; his life was disastrous, and soon the cousin's existence became catastrophic as she fought her mother's treachery. The Norman Rockwell façade was quickly crumbling.

There were temporary moments of escape during the long decade. Books provided the most consistent solace; I escaped into happy families, foreign countries, magical journeys. . .and found consolation. There were additional avenues out of the treachery of life at the aunts; I soon realized that music, a constant in that house, soothed anxiety, and muffled the arguments. Broadway tunes, the Ink Spots, Big Bands and Hogie Carmichael created an illusion of harmony.

Coastal Texas was a virtual garden, and the vibrant flowers in the yards, and the filled vases throughout the house took away some of the starkness of the cousin's hand-me-downs and ill fitting shoes.

Gourmet fare was a daily event. Weekend trips to the fishing boats assured that the freshest seafood was a staple. A beautifully set table with the best culinary offerings from the state honed my palette and guaranteed that I would learn to cook.

The house was pristine, and the order provided ways to navigate the quicksand of the emotional ambiance. It was an ongoing paradox: the farce of the "Norman Rockwell" family and the underlying dangers. Tempers were explosive, and while I was the most frequent target, the aunt and uncle sparred verbally with vicious words and heightened tempo. The cousin and her mother became increasingly estranged through the years, and their arguments eventually became violent.

It was essential to seek safe ground in that environment. The more I sought haven in my books, the greater the cousin's resentment. To establish the beloved daughter was favored, the aunt began to restrict my reading time. She took away my flashlight, limited the number of books I could take from the library, and forced me outside to spend time with the cousin. I soon became adept at hiding beloved titles under my blouses until safely out of view.

In first grade, I made friends. They were never allowed to visit at the aunts, but they were my school pals and frequent book buddies. One had a grandmother in the aunt's neighborhood, and I was occasionally allowed to walk there.

The mantra for the household was to appear normal, happy and in harmony. . .and for years that pretense was accepted by many. Years later I was told by my maternal grandmother, my parents closest friends, and a favorite uncle, that they were all aware of how unjust my life was in that family, but no one dared to confront the aunt.

So it was in superficial ways that I sought safety: the vicarious living through others' stories, the harmonious tunes on the record player, visual delight in nature and art, the development of a sophisticated palette, but consistently, and most vitally, in my conversations with God.

Time is an elusive factor, it seems as though there is too much, or not enough. The agony of the days and the chore of navigating the terrain became a daily goal. And so, I moved through first, second, and third grades seeing school as my safe haven, and losing myself in the world of fictional characters, academic successes and always, prayer.

Somehow, I made it to fourth grade, and one of the "angels among us" appeared as my teacher. It was her first teaching assignment, and she wanted her students to know that she cared. Within a few weeks, Mrs. Flynn handed me a typed contract that we held to throughout the school year. She outlined a daily schedule that permitted me to read and/or write once I had completed the requirements for that day. The stories and plays that I penned entertained the class on rainy days. In addition, she embellished my library by bringing me books from her home. It was a year of growth; I became an "author" and I had a grownup friend.

Fifth grade was terribly disappointing. I was no longer the class author encouraged by the loving teacher. My discomfort was heightened by the fact that my sweet, artistic fifth grade teacher offered no academic challenges. School no longer provided an opportunity to disconnect from the pain of day-to-day life. Despite the disappointments, I was still able to submerge myself in books and writing, and I did like and trust Mrs. Barr. She was kind, and encouraged students to express themselves through visual art; she did not, however, view writing as an art form.

During a particularly painful episode at the aunts, I confided in this kind teacher. I outlined the plight I faced daily, and as an advocate, she immediately contacted the aunt. The results were disastrous. The aunt assured her that I lied chronically, and that I was void of gratitude for all that she had sacrificed in order to provide a home for me. She painted a picture of a conniving, manipulative child. The teacher's support was withdrawn, from fear of the aunt or belief in the fabricated descriptions. I, of course, was severely punished.

At this juncture, disciplinary measures had moved from willow switches and deprivation of meals to confiscation of my books, hours in isolation (a cherished time) and always proclamations of my infractions. The analogies of my father and me grew. . .

During this time of confusion and dread I talked to God constantly, petitioning, crying, beseeching. . .I wanted out; my books were no longer enough.

LOSING ANCHORS

The monster within grew
There was a abyss within so terrifying that I could not admit it
To myself, to God
Would acknowledging the fear empower the monster
Would my Heavenly Father abandon me if I told Him of my darkness?
A father's legacy, violence
The hatred I had for the aunt, the cousin, the parents who deserted
Strangled me with terror of blood, loud noises, anger, guns, myself
Could I turn into my father?

The confusion became more intense as the precarious tightrope of life kept me forever on guard. The aunt was a "pillar" at the Presbyterian Church where she was lauded for her kindness toward the troubled, belligerent orphan taken into her home. The façade was difficult as the aunt delineated the long list of infractions I had logged each previous week.

The uncle avoided conflict with the aunt, and sought solace in his punching bag and workshop. As I learned decades later, there were others who witnessed the abuse first-hand, but did nothing to intervene. For some, it was a choice that followed them throughout their lives.

On some level, I began to believe some of the aunt's defining char-acterizations, i.e. I was homely, lazy (because I would rather read than play with the cousin), ungrateful. . .and as this list expanded, the aunt's delineation of her generosity grew. It was only after my escape at age sixteen did I learn that I had a bank account which covered all of my expenses, including food.

My lack of gratitude resulted in harsher treatment through the years, and so deprivation of adequate resources, such as shoes that fit, appropriately fitted clothing rather than her daughter's hand-me-downs (our bodily shapes were dichotomous), hygiene items during teen years, became part of her control.

LOST

Tisha, an auburn dachshund, belonging to "Aunt Mildy" and "Uncle Joe," gave birth to six puppies the summer of 1961. I was allowed to choose my puppy, a beautiful black and tan boy I named Oliver (Twist). Finally I had unconditional love.

As I cried for my parents, for the unjustness of the past seven years, for the lies. . .I also harbored tremendous hope. My brother was firmly established as part of the family friends' household. They were forced to answer my ongoing questions as I pleaded for information. Oliver was the proof that they cared for me. Surely if they took in my brother, they would allow me to join them and become a part of their family.

Those summer months were blurred by the rawness of confronting the lies buried for seven years. There were nightmares, tears and hours of questions as I shadowed my brother, and clung to Oliver. August loomed, and so did the arrival of the aunt. She came to fetch me back to Texas. Although I was terrified of challenging her, the anger and hatred that I harbored for her, fortified me. I began my litany of grievances as she was crossing the threshold. My promises of vengeance, expressions of pure hatred for living with years of lies, unbridled rage at the life she had inflicted on me were delineated.

Despite the terror I expressed at returning to that psychological prison, I was sent off, without Oliver.

Where was God in this? Why had He allowed the lies to perpetuate for seven long years? Why was I herded back to a place of danger and fear? Where was God? Where was Oliver?

PURGATORY

DEFINING HELL

I know what Hell is
I have been there
In the deep recesses of my mind
Frozen with fear
Consumed by darkness
Sickened by corruption
Without God
Too marred to accept His unconditional love
Too insecure to find Him in my shadows
Too frightened of His grace
Hell, a world without God
He never moves away, I do
And I seek other gods. . .
He waits patiently
Embraces the soiled child
Slays my dragons
Resurrects, cleans, heals
I am His!

The dictionary definitions of Hell are numerous and voluminous; I know it to be any state where God is not present. It was in that condition that I returned to Texas, void of God's constant comfort, divorced of the solace of school, scarred and scared. God did not abandon me, I negated Him. Hatred, anger, raw pain at the injustices consumed me, and so I turned my back on the Love that had sustained me through the trauma of the murder/suicide and the years with the abusive aunt. My prayers for deliverance were not answered, so I believed that once again I had been abandoned, this time by God.

The vacuum in which I found myself was horrifying. My bitterness erupted in litanies of life's unfairness, demands for freedom from the impossible situation in which I existed: I hated the aunt, and the aunt hated me. Once the Pandora's box was opened, I screamed against the careful fabrications that had been carefully constructed so that the world would not judge the aunt, or her deceased sister. I was afraid of my rage, afraid for my future, and without hope.

I now know that even as God pursues us, we can build defenses against His love, and that these walls are strongholds for Satan; he uses them to fan our fears, insecurities, anger. . .to attempt to thwart the reality of God's constant presence. It was during the following two years that I resided in a dark hole, seeing no possible exit.

The daily situation in which I existed was unbearable; the aunt could not let me go for fear of what I would reveal, and she no longer was able to control me with punishments and threats. As I focused on the tragedy of my plight, the marriage to #7 was unraveling, and the cousin was rebelling in dangerous ways. Nightly, she would escape the controlling restrictions her mother outlined, and she would leave for unknown adventures with nameless men. The bedroom window was the portal to freedom. Threats to kill me if I told, coupled with my distain for her, kept me quiet.

The pretense of harmony in that house dissolved as the aunt and uncle sparred; he retreated to the garage to pound the punching bag, and she escaped into her books. The cousin disappeared for hours at a time, and I cowered alone, afraid, no longer turning to God or to books.

Then a climax occurred that rewrote my world. One dreadful morning the cousin threw a butcher knife at her mother. She missed. The aunt viciously attacked me, claiming that I had turned her daughter against her. The slap to my face was so forceful that the imprint remained throughout the school day.

It was that afternoon that God broke through my resistance, He directed me to take the school bus to the minister's house. I do not recall having been there before, I only know that I was guided to that door. He was surprised to see me, and I believe that he only vaguely knew who I was. The bruise on my face, my outline of abuse, and my refusal to return to that home prompted a call. The uncle responded, corroborated my story, and asked to speak with me. Begging forgiveness for standing aside during my decade of abuse at the hands of his wife, he pledged safety if I would return to finish the academic year. He promised protection and an exit.

THE TRAIN NORTH

THE EXIT

The agonizing loneliness of stepping into the passenger section of the train

Gripping my sole suitcase, filled with books

I had dreamed, prayed, and planned for this moment for ten years

To be free of the aunt

Never to be subject to her cruelty again

When the moment came, I was afraid to take it

I would board the train and head north

To a brother I did not know

To a new sister-in-law who would not welcome me

I climbed the steps to the passengers' coach to escape

Alone and unwanted at sixteen

I understood fear, it had permeated every waking moment for ten long years

Fear of death, of guns, the aunt's anger, her daughter's threats

Fear of rejection

Tommy did not want me, he was newly married

The family friends were too old to take in a sixteen year old

Boarding school, an orphanage, or the minister's house. . .on a trial basis

Loneliness.

And so it was that I was deposited on the sidewalk in front of a parsonage. The family friends did not accompany me to the door; they did admonish me to be grateful, while delineating how fortunate I was that this couple was willing to take in a "troubled" teen. I was completely baffled by the family friends I had known all of my life; they left me on a sidewalk, alone, without an explanation (that came years later. . .). With trepidation, I knocked on the front door of the Quaker parsonage, and was admitted by the minister's wife. She made it overtly clear that this was a trial, the last teen they had taken in lasted three months.

I was led to a small, Spartan upstairs bedroom with a window overlooking the backyard. The minister's wife then left me with no outline of expectations, protocol, or schedules. My memory of that Sunday afternoon is one of intense sadness for the vulnerable sixteen year old orphan, again on quicksand.

Watching from the upstairs window I saw the minister walk through the yard. I prayed for kindness, safety and stability. On that heartbreaking afternoon my hopes were again in limbo.

As that summer unfolded life was paradoxical. The aunt's adamant versions of the ten years under her tutelage were painted with the image of a lying, manipulative teen, and unfortunately, the guardians fully accepted her explanations for "why she could no longer have me under her roof." I was required to write her weekly; the minister's wife edited the correspondence and disregarded my pleas to divorce myself from the abuser.

The church family, however, threw energy and passion into making me feel welcomed and safe, and I was soon adopted by a congregation. God's daily presence again loomed as I experienced Him through the kindnesses of the parishioners. My wardrobe was replenished by a young mother in the church; she loved to sew and sought out patterns appropriate for a high school student. The organist offered babysitting jobs so that I could have spending money. The Youth Group welcomed me with enthusiasm, and provided tutorials for the upcoming school year. And, the two small daughters of the guardians followed me everywhere begging for books to be read aloud, shoes to be tied. . .Slowly, and I believe despite their intentions, the guardians let their defenses down and accepted me into their home.

Success at school was paramount; the minister was on the local school board. Active participation in Sunday School, meeting for worship, and Youth Group was expected. By the time I entered my junior year in high school, I had a community; it was not a family, and I always knew that acceptance was contingent, but I accepted a degree of security, and even popularity.

The high school program was academically challenging and stimulating. I took Russian Literature, Russian Language and Russian History, discovered Tolstoy, Dostoyevsky, and Chekhov, and in the process once again sought solace, guidance and hope vicariously through the lives of others.

It was during this transformative time in my life that I began to think more deeply about God. That November the Youth Group travelled to New York City for a four day retreat. As young Quakers, we attended sessions at the United Nations on world peace, visited the Automat and the Statue of Liberty, and worshipped at a Friends Meeting near the youth hostel in which we were housed.

It was in that small, austere house of worship that God spoke to me directly. On a grey, rainy November morning, with the deep fatigue of travel settling in, the chirp of a small bird perched on a limb brushing the meeting house window claimed my attention. Just at the moment the tiny creature gained my attention, a shaft of sunlight broke through the grey morning, illuminating God's messenger. Somehow I knew that moment was orchestrated just for me, and I knew that my loving Father had indeed boarded that Texas train!

BOOK TWO

Metamorphose

The physical transformation I embraced that first year was dramatic. The metal braces that had hindered my smile for five years were removed. I left the corrective shoes and the heavy inserts on the train. My 5'5" frame began to develop, and the unruly orange hair that had been my nemesis took shape. I emerged as a reasonably attractive teenager with beautiful teeth and a new attitude.

The primary metamorphosis during the two years with the guardians was emotional; fear was no longer the pervading reaction. I found a community of Christian friends, academically engaged, and socially popular. We spent a lot of time together, much of it at the parsonage. Friday night curfew for most of us was 10:00, dates were allowed in for pizza and ice cream until 11:00. The guys were sent scurrying, and the girls spent hours giggling and planning the next events. Dates were squeaky clean; we went skate boarding and ice skating as a group, visited the county fair and the dairy bar in packs. It was an era of simple values, and I later realized that again, it was God at the helm, placing me in a circle of safety.

Youth group was core to our social activities, and we held long, serious discussions about faith, the virgin birth, Christ's walk with us, the future. . .no one I knew drank, smoked, cussed, or engaged in sexual intimacy. The fellowship of those friends provided sound parameters delineating what was acceptable behavior and for me it was a needed structure. A child without roots, I was strengthened by the wise choices of my friends.

We were invested in high school basketball (it was Indiana in the 1960s), sock hops, cheer block, school clubs, house parties chaperoned by caring adults; it was "Mayberry U.S.A.," and I was so fortunate to be hundreds of miles away from the tragedies unfolding in Texas.

The spring of my senior year, the uncle killed himself, the cousin was pregnant and unmarried, and I had no relationship with my big brother, although he lived just thirty miles away. These intrusions into that respite from fear were reminders that the future loomed, uncertain. . .

HOPE

The group was headed to Indiana University, and I was delegated to a small Quaker college in the "Hog Belt" of Ohio farm country. Missing my friends, and once again alone, I arrived on campus for Freshman Orientation, the fall of 1966. It was a traditionally beautiful college setting with acres of land, brick buildings and tree lined sidewalks. The ambiance was solid, and provided a sense of warmth and welcome. Family style meals furthered the perception of community.

America was at war, torn apart because of the conflict in Vietnam. The Civil Rights Movement, headed by Dr King, was attracting the attention of college students nationwide. The "Hippies" were touting free love and shared liberties, and the college was a miniscule reflection of the times. There were students enlisting, others avoiding the draft, protesters of the war, followers of Dr. King, and some with allegiance to Malcolm X. Drugs were available, as was flower power.

It was in this arena that I met my best friend, Ivan. I found that Ivan was one of the few early morning breakfast attendees. We soon began to share that breakfast hour, as we have for the past fifty-five years. Our conversations were diverse as we spoke of his athletic prowess (Mid-Ohio Conference for two consecutive years as an offensive guard), politics, religion, and of course, my boyfriend, Ivan's roommate.

Divine intervention was again put into place on my behalf. The roommate had to return to Connecticut to work on his grade point average. Promising to return, he asked Ivan to take care of me until his parents permitted him to rejoin the campus community. Ivan, a person of absolute integrity, a Christian with a fundamental faith, an athlete, student. . .this is the man that I believe was placed in my world by an ever watchful Heavenly Father.

LOVE

Rides through the country on his Bridgestone bike
Picnics with his family
Mugs of hot tea and mounds of butter pecan ice cream
Forums for sharing
We talked of life, faith, the world, hopes, dreams. . .
We fell in love without intending for it to happen,
And we just keep falling. . .

RESISTENCE

The guardians were enthralled with the work ethics of the young man I introduced as my platonic friend. A first generation college student, Ivan was paying his way through a work/study program, entailing factory work three days a week, classes three days a week, coupled with football practice, studying, Greek life activities, and campus leadership. It was an impressive resume. There were many similarities to the minister's undergraduate days, when he arrived at a small Quaker college in Indiana just off the farm. He too worked, played football, and maintained an active social life. There was a friendly simpatico relationship that was shattered months later when we announced our engagement.

The guardians in their plans for me, had selected the young Quaker with whom I was to spend the rest of my life, and it was not Ivan. By then, the guardian had secured a position as a college dean, and was thoroughly committed to orchestrating my life to demonstrate that their tutelage with me had been successful. Their choice was in truth my platonic friend; he was a wonderful, committed member of The Society of Friends, with aspirations to serve in the Peace Corp. I admired him immensely, loved him as a friend, but I was not in love with him.

On the other hand, Ivan and I had a friendship based on shared values that had slowly moved from the platonic relationship we shared for well over a year, to include the deep love designed by God for husbands and wives.

MARCH 16, 1968

The day that forever redefined my life, my idea of family and my hopes for the future was met with paradoxical reactions. The guardian's wife declared that she would give us six months. One of the selected members of my wedding party made it clear that I would never be forgiven for selecting Ivan over the guardian's choice. Rain poured, forecasting a very bad hair day. It was mid-March, cold and dreary. Within hours the sun broke through, the temperatures rose, and so did the promises of a glorious day for a wedding.

In a historic Quaker Meeting House, Ivan and I promised to love and to cherish forever. God was in that moment.

CINDERELLA DOES NOT EXIST, GOD IS SO MUCH BIGGER THAN DISNEY

Dictionaries define acclimation as a psychological adjustment. In 1968, I became a member of a family after fourteen tenuous years. Marriage ushered in a world that had only existed in the pages of my beloved books. I was wanted, without contingencies. This was a time of dreams realized and of tremendous insecurities about the permanency of family, of happiness and of safety.

Initially we settled into a tiny apartment adjacent to the college football field. With no funds for a honeymoon, we planned to spend the freedom of Spring Break moving into our new shared space; God had other plans. A late spring snow storm turned the college campus into a wonderland. We took walks, laughed and played. It was an idyllic beginning.

Within weeks our family expanded; we brought home a ten week old German Shepherd puppy, and christened him Jasper. From the beginning, Jasper was remarkable. His classic silver and black markings, keen intelligence and affectionate nature captivated us. So we became a family of three.

In addition to our beautiful canine, we extended our clan to include college friends and Ivan's siblings and parents. Ivan prepared for graduation by completing student teaching, and I learned to cook. From this safe cocoon we learned that real life always intervenes: Dr. Martin Luther King, Jr. was assassinated; his death rocked our college community and our idealism. Bobby Kennedy's tragic death within a few weeks punctuated the fact that life cannot be lived in isolation.

Transitions are frequently wrought with insecurities, facing the unknown is an act of courage (Campbell, Joseph 1990). Moving from the dangers of life in Texas to the probationary status of the guardians was an acclimation. The journey from high school to a small Quaker college was another required adjustment. It was marriage, however, that demanded the greatest leap of faith. There had been few models of trust, family and/or love. . .I had been abandoned by the most trusted, my parents. Those early years of marriage were noteworthy for it was during that time that I came to know that my intelligent, handsome husband was a man of absolute, unbendable integrity. The moral yardstick that Ivan embodied was based in his faith, the examples set by his parents, and the deeply embedded qualities of honesty and fair play. This foundation both provided the foundation of security I so desperately sought, and it provided a daily window into God's constant involvement in my life.

As we learned to be "Mr. and Mrs. Cooper," traditions were formed that have continued through five plus decades. Holding hands and praying before each meal was a comforting way to acknowledge God's generosity and presence. Fresh flowers, music, and candlelight set the ambiance for a couple seeking ways to express love for one another. Daily notes placed in Ivan's lunchbox expressed my appreciation of his love, of God's goodness and the miracle of us. During this time we attended church erratically, called upon divine intervention during crises, and lived as though we were invincible. It was not that we overtly put our faith walk on hold, we just got too busy learning to be a family. God, however, did not budge, and continued to navigate our journey in dramatic ways.

Shortly after Ivan's graduation, we settled into a modest rental within walking distance of Ivan's parents' home. Ivan found employment at Ruthman Machinery Company, where he was promised opportunities within the office. It was a family affair; Ivan's father, brother, and brother-in-law were also Ruthman employees.

I secured work as a secretary, and began a quest to find a teaching position for Ivan. After all, I had married a teacher. . .

We purchased a tent and began to camp, spent most of our time socializing with Ivan's family, and delighting in Jasper, and each other.

Christmas loomed as the event of our first year of marriage. Sequins, unadorned foam balls, felt, and patterns filled the small house as we crafted stockings, ornaments, and a tree. Shopping, baking, wrapping gifts, and mailing cards filled the weeks between Thanksgiving and Christmas. It was a memorable time, filled with family and friends.

As we planned our first wedding anniversary celebrations, I continued to send Ivan's resume to every Quaker school in the United States. My reasoning was that an education degree from a Friends college would pave the way. He received two invitations to interview; the prestigious Sidwell Friends School, and Moorestown Friends in New Jersey asked for on-site reviews of his credentials. So, on the eve of our anniversary, Ivan drove east to explore the possibilities. He was not able to locate Sidwell Friends, so he drove north to New Jersey. Once again the Lord was intervening on our behalf, and Ivan returned to Kentucky with a new job as a teacher.

At Ohio's oldest inn, The Golden Lamb, we celebrated a year richly blessed by God. We discovered that Charles Dickens had been a guest at the inn, and that it was the site of a Victorian Christmas celebration. It became the place to go for every meaningful event, and over the decades the memories of the special first anniversary were firmly tied to The Golden Lamb.

With naïve eagerness, we prepared to move to the densely populated town of Cherry Hill, New Jersey. Real estate was way too costly for young married couples, plus we had to find lodging that would not only accept, but welcome, our third family member, Jasper. High rise apartments were being constructed in Cherry Hill, and one was a "pets" facility. With incredible excitement we moved into a modern facility, with a dishwasher! The balcony provided a view of a distant drive-in movie theatre, so without sound, we could enjoy contemporary shows for free. The ambiance was simpatico; among the interesting "pet parents" were a pilot and his wife, an oil heiress. They quickly offered their friendship; they had just lost their German Shepherd, and they embraced Jasper, and us. We were introduced to fine wines, four course gourmet meals, flights in their small Cherokee plane, and a life new to us. It was a learning experience.

It was a time of turmoil in America, and Moorestown Friends School did not escape. At the end of the academic year, 43 full-time faculty members left their positions for philosophical reasons. The institution seemed to have shed the Quaker traditions, and there was instability. We headed back to Kentucky and Ivan's family; however, a summer of "camping out" in his parents' basement sent us scurrying for privacy and employment. It was much later that we recognized that once again God had redirected our course.

Ivan quickly found an opening in the Kenton County, Kentucky school system, and I was hired to work as a secretary for a psychological consulting firm. We located a home for rent in a pleasant neighborhood and once again acclimated.

Christmas was the focal point of our holiday celebrations, and that third year of our marriage we decided to host the family gathering. Twenty Coopers gathered for a feast of standing rib roast and Yorkshire pudding, but few would venture into our culinary discoveries of British fare; it was not a successful hosting. We did, however, follow-up with a New Year Eve party that was attended by friends and family as we celebrated life together.

The summer of 1971 was a turning point in our young marriage. Ivan's only sister left her husband and moved into our rented home with her three year old daughter. During that summer we boarded Jasper and returned to New Jersey to visit a dear friend and former colleague from Moorestown. One week later we returned to Kentucky to discover that Jasper was dead. The grief, anger, hurt, and confusion permeated every waking moment. We turned to God for answers, and through the long months He provided solace from memories, and a medical autopsy that determined a dormant virus had rapidly and painlessly taken him. And, Jasper had just fathered a litter of puppies, so we took the "pick." We brought Pilgrim home, not to replace Jasper, but to carry on his tradition of love, loyalty and intelligent companionship; he was his father's son!

The intimate reconnect with God was overdue, but so crucial in honing us as we moved forward. God at the parameters had not anchored us, but God, emphatically back in the center, did. He, of course, had just been waiting for our invitation.

It was at this juncture that we began to seriously search for tangible roots: a home. Within months we found what can only be described as "God's real estate." On his way to a school related meeting, Ivan got lost in rural Kenton County, *and just happened* to see a "**FOR SALE**" sign in the yard of a large Edwardian home. He arrived home assuring me that I would love the home he had "happened" on that day. With tremendous excitement I called the number listed, and spoke at length with the owner; as we conversed, I realized that she was the wife of one of Ivan's colleagues. My excitement waned as soon as the asking price was related, and even though she insisted that we should visit, I hung up disappointed. It was several weeks later that I saw an ad in the newspaper for a farmhouse in the country; I called. To discover that it was the Edwardian, still on the market, was another disappointment until the owner insisted that we visit to discuss options. The two and a half storied structure was white clapboard, with a large leaded glass window adjacent to the front door. The front porch was covered, and the twenty-two 81 inch windows gave the house a welcoming, airy ambiance.

The wallpaper, curling to the floor, did not deter our enthusiasm. Black and white floor titles in the kitchen, a "laundry room" in the basement, no closets just two pressers (areas between walls in which to store and "press" clothing items) did nothing to deter our joy in discovering this gem; we had found a magical site, a dream with unlimited potential. The owners just wanted to keep 83 of the 84 acres, and discard the old house. So we purchased our

"Rockwell" dream for $24,000 and spent the next 24 years living and growing as we refurbished.

Throughout these early years my Heavenly Father was strengthening and preparing me for the inevitable confrontation with my past. It was essential to revisit the tragedies of my childhood in order to illuminate how God's love uses those wounds to heal us and others (Rohr, 2011).

STABILITY

Stability took on the illusion of permanence as we settled into our Edwardian house in rural Kenton County, Kentucky. Surrounded by over eighty acres, with cows as the nearest neighbors, it was a picturesque setting. The house had been vacant for several years, and was in need of a great deal of cosmetic work; the grounds were lovely, and overlooked pastures of cows, tobacco fields, and gardens. The neighbors were farmers, attentive, but proudly independent. It was the ideal respite to grow roots and become anchored. The landscape shouted of God's majesty, and His presence was evident in the ponds, woods, wildlife. . .and the simplicity of a rural lifestyle; it was medicinal. I discovered God in the woods beyond the barn, on the log bench beside the pond, in the gentle bay of the cows and the frolicking energy of the colt. The natural beauty fed my soul, and I began to find God in miniscule events and unexpected places; the serenity of a lifestyle that was primarily focused on a loving Father, each other, and our beloved German Shepherd, Pilgrim, and allowed me to believe that safety was possible.

Ivan's parents were an integral part of those years; they loved me without qualification. I began to believe that happiness could be permanent, and that my life was blessed. We taught elementary school, grew a large organic garden, collected stray cats and adopted abandoned Scotties, found a church home, refurbished the Edwardian, spent quality time with Ivan's family, and found harmony. . .for awhile.

Too soon our cocoon unraveled. The premature, unexpected death of Ivan's beloved father redefined our world. A man of great warmth and love of family, he was a beacon around which we gathered weekly for home cooked meals, card games and laughter. Ivan's mother was the pragmatic core of the family, an accomplished baker and the family cook, she ran the details of the family home while his father provided the whimsical spirit of fun. We were devastated by the loss of this man who had provided a strong work ethic, demonstrated love of family overtly, celebrated Christmas with passion and always found laughter.

Initially the vacuum he left was filled with the immediate tasks of providing support for Ivan's mother, and securing her financial security. As she settled into life without her husband of forty-three years, new routines developed. Ivan assumed the responsibility of caretaker of the old house in which she lived; he also oversaw all of the paper work required to keep her there. I began to call her every afternoon to report on the happenings in my sixth grade classroom, Ivan's teaching and coaching activities, plans to see her during the weekend and to assure her of our love. It was a connection we both cherished for the following decade.

We had been given years of stability, happiness, health, and hope. . .but sometime during the period of grief for Ivan's dad, the nightmares began. I would awake at 3:23 a.m., drenched, terrified, and uncertain of the cause. With a racing heart, fear that defied definition and a foreboding sense of danger, I called out to God and to Ivan. My journey into the dark hole of hopelessness stripped all sense of joy and safety from life. I muddled through the days, teaching, pretending that all was normal, and only Ivan and I knew the depth of my despair. We sought help from Christian professionals, and began the long walk of reliving the years of abuse at the hand of the aunt, and the fears that had consumed much of my childhood. The five year odyssey from serious depression to glorious healing was a faith walk that we trekked together; Ivan held my hand, promised that we would get to the other side and supported me unequivocally.

Midway through this dark period, I was diagnosed with probable cancer (it followed six prior surgeries for cysts that had been benign); the tumor grew so quickly that I was advised to "get my papers in order." Throughout this ordeal we sought God, and shortly before the scheduled surgery we experienced "divine intervention." I woke Ivan up at 3 a.m. to announce that I had experienced a vision. In it, I was walking through a field of wildflowers, and I was greeted by our first German Shepherd, Jasper, Ivan's father, my maternal grandmother. . .none spoke. . .as I continued through the field a powerful, but caressing voice said, "You are not ready to leave Ivan, go home and write." Ivan's first question was how I was going to write God, quickly followed by, "Oh, you are supposed to work on your writing." At that point we knew that I was going to survive the surgery; God had plans for our future (Jeremiah 29:11).

This intimate reminder of God's love and intervention did not immediately pull me out of depression. I was aware that He had a purpose for me, and that was reassuring, but I was still battling the demons of doubt, fear, anxiety, "what ifs."..and so the Christian counseling continued. Prayer, Bible study, and begging and petitioning God were constant components of each day as I desperately sought safety again. Love for Ivan and God thwarted the ongoing thoughts of suicide; I wanted to finally be at peace, free from fear, but I was too afraid to be without Ivan or God to act on thoughts of escape.

There were powerful messages from Christian writers that provided lifelines, Catherine Marshall's examination of grief after the loss of her beloved husband, Peter Marshall, Corrie ten Boon's forgiveness of those who had imprisoned her, and so many others, allowed me to trust enough. It was finally through the act of prayer, affirming God's healing love, that I released my past into my Lord's hands, and with shaky knees walked into the future. Daily praise prayers, thanking my Heavenly Father, Jesus, and the Holy Spirit for restoring me built renewed hope and moved me off quicksand and onto solid ground.

It is important to note that reliving childhood tragedies as an adult is a complex and deeply frightening endeavor. For me, the pain of the child was seen through two lens, that of an adult, and that of the victimized child. I am quite sure that I could not have moved through that deep chasm without the love of the Lord, and the support of Ivan. Richard Rohr's (2011) urging to let God use our wounds to heal us and to help others is vitally important. The healing is a life-giving answer from our heavenly Father, but the sharing of it is our gift to others who need to know that although we are powerless, He is not!

Depression is not isolated to psychological hopelessness; it depletes spiritual strength, physical health, and unfortunately impacts those who most love you in multiple ways. Ivan's anger that he could not "fix" me, was replaced with vicarious pain for what I was suffering. For five long years he slugged through the daily valleys with me, vacillating from frustration to determination, always sure that we would get to a better place. As we looked toward the future, we soon discovered that God had not only healed me, He had amazing plans for us. . .

GOD'S SURPRISES

Even now, after 75 years of unscripted living, I am amazed at how exactly my heavenly Father orchestrated my path. The kaleidoscope reflecting the journey is brilliant with light permeating the darkness. Knowing that out of the ashes the Phoenix rises directs me to walk through the depths and to embrace transformation.

I did not choose teaching. I believe that I was directed into the classroom. The initial venture began with an invitation to teach kindergarten in the basement of the Baptist Church in Dayton, Kentucky. The year was 1974. The sole criteria I had: the willingness to embrace the opportunity. Without a college degree and no prior courses in education, I readily signed a contract to teach 25 children for an academic year.

After 40 years in a variety of classrooms, I continue to acknowledge that initial experience was my educational "swan song." What I did not know about curriculum and instruction freed me to explore learning for the pure joy of it! We played, parents joined us daily. . .we sang, wrote stories, read volumes of books, drew, investigated the surrounding neighborhood and we became a community. It was an invigorating, life-changing year.

There were no coloring books, ditto skill pages, or programmed curricula; we "winged" it. Each day I read carefully chosen books aloud, displaying print and illustrations. Responses came in the forms of discussions, pictures, and written tales of their own. We marched through the small town counting sidewalk squares, red doors, houses, trees, people wearing blue. . .and we learned. I soon realized that each child brought something uniquely theirs to broaden our group, and in the process, I discovered that magic of watching them bloom.

Just as Ivan and I recognized that God was redirecting me, and that it was time to return to college to obtain the teaching degree, the Kindergarten Board summoned me. I was required to explain why children in pre-school were reading, writing and completing first grade mathematical equations. A curriculum founded on joyful learning was unveiled, and the Board that had intended to fire me, offered a new contract. God, however, was beaconing. . .

I studied diligently, and tested out of 45 hours of undergraduate courses, challenged three additional classes, and was able to complete the degree program in two years, graduating with recognition as "The Outstanding Student in Early Childhood Education," (Northern Kentucky University, Class of 1977). Step-by-step, God was pushing, goading and supporting in measurable ways.

While student teaching I was called into the principal's office. I recall entering with trepidation, concerned that I had committed some infraction. Instead, I was offered a teaching position for the fall. It was the beginning of a nine year partnership with Kenton Elementary where I taught sixth grade for five years, and kindergarten twice a day for two years, and then began a new career path. Mornings were spent at Northern Kentucky University where I taught Literature for Children and afternoons were in the kindergarten arena at Kenton. It was a dichotomy that enriched all of us. At that time, I also began to take doctoral level courses at the University of Cincinnati. The importance of those years had much to do with the people God placed in my path.

By 1978, Ivan joined the Kenton faculty, and we were able to teach "together" for eight years. Blessed by a progressive administrator, who trusted us to make sound curriculum decisions, we were free to be innovative. By that time, I was deeply immersed in Holistic Education, using real literature, authentic writing forums and relevant life experiences to hone skills. The students soared academically and were validated by standardized test scores.

I was offered the opportunity to teach graduate students for Northern Kentucky University in London, England during a five week session. Ivan was able to accompany me on our first international adventure. The course, One Hundred Years of British Literature for Children, was additional evidence of God's ever present involvement. I had treasured Dickens throughout my childhood because of his depictions of "lost" children, and I was in his territory. In addition to exploring the literature, the twelve graduate students, Ivan and I visited Holistic schools, met with authors and illustrators, read voraciously, engaged in lively book discussions, and grew. I returned to Kentucky a zealot for educational reform.

The students under my tutelage shaped the curriculum and instruction as I continued to examine options to "skill and drill" programs. The backing of the building principal allowed me to experiment. It was, however, always the students who directed the dance.

Year one at Kenton Elementary was a time of exciting growth. I met Paul, a transfer student and an orphan. Our bond was immediate. His deep need to delve into academics as a coping mechanism was something I understood. We stayed in touch for decades, and our last visit in the 1990s occurred when he was on leave as a Naval Commander.

Year three brought unexpected challenges, the best being a large group of academically gifted students who spurred one another. It was that term that I met a young man with an insatiable yearning for knowledge. He, too, had a tragic story and lived in a tenuous environment. I was excited by the prospect of keeping his keen mind engaged, and thoroughly enjoyed his need to know. Slowly, this unusual pre-teen found a place in the peer group as he was mentored by an unusual classmate. The friend who ushered this inquisitive boy into a world of social mores was a gifted student, but also an athlete, poet (Kentucky State Award) and overt Christian. For the first time, the "nerdy" outcast was accepted for who he was. I continue to correspond these many years later with both of these former students from whom I learned so much.

That third year was idyllic. The students excelled in an open-ended curriculum, exceeded state expectations, bonded and supported one another in the classroom and on the basketball court (they won the Kenton County Championship), and they taught their "teacher" volumes.

As frequently happens after a peak, the following year resembled a plateau. There were, of course, exceptional students, but as a group they never formed a community. The excitement of the pure joy of learning was missing. . .

It was time to ponder where God wanted me next. The principal asked if I would be willing to move from sixth grade to the newly formed kindergarten program; he wanted to place Ivan in the upper level class as a male model of discipline and integrity. I was promised academic freedom.

Using the models I had observed in the United Kingdom, I began an exciting Holistic Kindergarten program. Five parents committed to daily roles in the classroom to facilitate a curriculum that was built around revolving learning centers. It was a jubilant success for the students and their parents! I kept copious notes on what worked and what needed to changed, and incorporated those the following years.

It was during this exciting period as an educator that I realized that once again God was directing me toward a dramatic change. I tendered my resignation the spring of 1986, and began a doctoral program in the College of Curriculum and Instruction at the University of Cincinnati.

Jeremiah 29:11 = Buck

EVOLUTION

He was seven
A waif
Afraid
In need
He found unconditional love
A forever home
He was nineteen when the past defined the future
The Air Force, a connection to his biological father
Once a poet
Now a warrior.

Oh, the plans that the Lord had (has) for us! The years, following my acceptance of God's healing, unfolded quickly. As stated previously, life is not linear, and the chronology of events is often interwoven into an overlapping tapestry.

Childless, and realizing that biological children were unlikely to be a part of the future, we threw our energies into teaching, and cherishing the children under our tutelage. It was then that we came to know a seven year old waif whose mother had died the previous year from cancer. This special child shared a home with three siblings, three cousins, his father and an aunt. They had no indoor plumbing, and the house stood directly across the street from the school in which we taught; it was apparent to the staff, faculty, administration, and students that there was deprivation.

The earliest recollection of the young boy who forever changed our lives was during his first grade tenure. I saw him in the hallway with his teacher; she was admonishing him to "look like he was in trouble" when he returned to the classroom. After school that day I asked her what infraction had elicited that exchange. She said that he was talkative and disruptive, but she did not have the heart to discipline him considering all that he had recently suffered. From that time, I took an active interest in "the boy." He was physically waif-like, but adorable, with beautiful eyes and an engaging grin. At every opportunity I spoke to him, trying to lighten his wounded heart.

In those days, Ivan painted classrooms during the summer to supplement our educators' salaries. One summer while painting at Kenton Elementary he discovered that he had a shadow/companion as he ventured from room to room. Buck wandered across the road each morning, and spent his days "helping" Ivan paint. Within a few days, Ivan called to ask whether I was "okay" with Buck coming to dinner. Of course I was! Permission obtained from his father, Buck accompanied Ivan home for his first introduction to our beloved German Shepherd, Pilgrim, a life style dichotomous to the one to which he was accustomed, and a family that found him intriguing. This initiated a pattern that fell into a rhythm. Buck became an integral part of our lives, and we cherished time with him. His father endorsed the relationship and was deeply appreciative of the attentiveness and time we had for his younger son.

During his years in elementary school, Buck took on a number of roles: a basketball player on Ivan's team, a student in Ivan's sixth grade class, and a frequent part of our family ventures. Graduation to middle school promoted him to the role of "coaching assistant" as he came each day to tutor the fifth and six graders playing basketball. He continued to participate in many of our extended activities, i.e. dinners to the Spaghetti Factory, Chi-Chi's Mexican Restaurant, Bob Evans, and of course, time in the country with us. We fell in love with this intelligent, caring child, and were deeply thankful that God placed him in our lives.

Buck's biological father loved him deeply, but was often engulfed in relationships that left too little time for extracurricular activities. His willingness to let us expand Buck's world, and his appreciation of the opportunities we provided were often verbalized. We had a "son" placed in our hearts: he was the very one we would have chosen, and his father had the assurance that his youngest boy was experiencing a life that opened vistas.

Four plus decades later the only relationships as precious to us are those with the Lord and each other. We love Buck perhaps more than we would have a biological child because we understand the miracle of God's intervention. He is an amazing, incredibly successful man, son, husband, father and servant of the Lord. Everyday we are deeply blessed by this unexpected gift set on our door by a Father who loves us.

To address the immediate transition from a depression so deep that I literally experienced Hell: separation from God, to a live fully defined in Jeremiah 29:11, I will address the miracles that follow. Buck headed that tangible result of prayers, but there were, and continue to be, so many others.

Buck

Our "son"
When you laugh, I smile
We talk, honestly, openly
So, why did you leave?
Why did you chose a risky career?
I love you without conditions
I miss you intensely
I need you. . .
I am sad, scared, angry.

Dear Buck,

You are constantly with me, sometimes at the forefront of my mind as I reel from the news reports, talk to God about you, and think about my multiple blessings, and sometimes you are relegated to the recesses of my thoughts as I strive to avoid fearful images. Questions flood my waking moments and haunt my dreams. The networks emphatically announce that Special Operation Teams are in Afghanistan, Iran, Iraq, Syria. . . Are you there? My heart is so weighted that I believe you must be. My "mom" perspective seems to be radar that alerts me when you are in harms' way. So many times during the years I have prayed for your safety without knowledge of your whereabouts. Buck, I am so proud of you, even when your choices put you at risk. An emotion even stronger than pride is love, and I love you selfishly—enough to want you home.

Kosovo was frightening, Bosnia scared me as much as North Korea, but this is different. Maybe you have done enough; I am icy with fear for your survival. I cannot bear to think of my world without your loving smile, teasing laugh, caring hugs. . .each time you are home we trace the journeys that made us family, and then build additional memories.

"Our son"
Does it matter that I am scared, not just for a moment, but every waking second?
Would you come home to ease my fears, if you could?
I am afraid that I will never hear you laugh again. Do you know how much I cherish the pure joy of your laughter?
What about the stories, our stories? Is there a legacy if you don't come home?
You are a poet, a writer, a dreamer, and an athletic. . .why war?
What can your sacrifice do to make sense of a world gone mad?
Come home.

THE CALL

"Good morning, I love you!"
The voice of the son deployed on the other side of the world.
He is coming home after three extensions
We have 13 hours
Then he will debrief
Have more special training
Return to where he cannot be reached, to where phone calls are erratic or non-existent
To his high security status, assuring me that he is always in danger
But for now, he will be home in 75 hours, and we will celebrate him, us, our family, love and safety, and we will try to pretend that he is home for good. . .

But, he loves the challenge of being Special Ops
He does his job so well
I have to let him go.

THE WALL

We walk hand in hand through the Vietnam Memorial
Reading names on the wall, noting memorabilia left as reminders of love
I tell him that I cannot read his name on a wall. . .he says that I would be proud
I ask him to promise not to ask that
So for now the tenseness is loosened

A DAUGHTER-IN-LAW

I am a Mother-in-Law! You are happy. . .
We are thankful grandparents!

THE PROMISE

Every phone call ends with "the promise": you will come home
We both know that it is in God's hands, and I continue to believe
I know that He always keeps His promises

BUCK

So far away geographically, so close to my heart always
What happened to the skinny boy who loved big time wrestling, bikes, and MacDonalds?
At 19 you became a soldier

At 21 you were sent to Japan
Fourteen years later you were a Sergeant in Special Operations,
in harms' way
That small child became a wonderful man, a son, a husband, a
father...
What did not change was my love for you, I merely exchanged
fear of bike wrecks for anxiety about international terrorists,
with the knowledge that my love cannot protect you, but God
can!

ANOTHER CHAPTER IN THE LIFE OF...

At Ivan's urging, I applied for a "full ride" to a doctoral program
at the University of Cincinnati. To get the needed scholarship and
annual stipend it was necessary to score in the top ten percent of
post-graduate applications across the nation. The morning of the
examination I was suffering from a sinus infection, Ivan's mother
was hospitalized with serious heart problems, and the lens of my
glasses were severely scratched. I entered the testing arena with
trepidation, knowing that we could not afford a doctoral degree.
Success on the test was the determining factor. Although I had
studied for the exams, I knew that the results were in God's hands.
Weeks later, the scores arrived in the mail; I had received a full
scholarship and a generous stipend as a doctoral candidate in the
College of Curriculum and Instruction at the University of Cincinnati. So a new chapter began...
I resigned from my teaching position in Kenton County, Kentucky
and began the pursuit of an advanced degree. Each time I read
God's Winks (Rushnell, 2001), I am reminded of the ways in which
God intervened, orchestrated, nudged, and directed my path
during this journey. I was offered an unprecedented position as
a full-time instructor at the university, with health benefits and
tuition. That opportunity also ushered in a group of mentors who
forever changed my life. The Chair of my Doctoral Committee, a
noteworthy scholar, championed me for the five years of course

work, written and oral exams, dissertation and successful defense. She was an amazing role model, friend, tutor, and advocate. I was buoyed by faculty, committee members, colleagues, pioneers in the field (international literature for children, adolescents, and young adults), and of course, Ivan and God. It was an invigorating process, and I am deeply grateful to the many who guided the journey.

The fall of 1988 was noteworthy; God winks were a daily occurrence, although I did not yet know the term. I was asked to interview at the University of Kentucky's Library College for a position teaching Children's Literature, (I was still taking doctoral course work), and I was invited to teach in an international program in England the summer of 1989. Initially I ignored the calls from the university; we had just lost Ivan's mother to heart disease after a long period of hospitalization. Exhaustion, grief, and the improbability of securing a tenure-track position in one of the nation's most prestigious library colleges while still taking courses made the follow up ridiculous. Over a period of weeks, phone messages urging that I call a prominent professor in the College of Library and Information Science at the University of Kentucky, showed up at the public library and a favorite bookstore. God does work in wondrous ways! The initial telephone conversation with that professor, who was to become a dear friend and Christian mentor, was simpatico; she was calling on behalf of her beloved friend, an icon in Children's Literature, who was retiring. After attending a presentation I had given at a Literature conference, she wanted me to interview.

On the eve of that engagement, I seriously considered calling it off; it was too improbable. Ivan encouraged me to go for the experience of interviewing, so off I ventured to meet one of my real life heroes, a legend in my field. It was a day of delight, interacting with two distinguished professors, but I left, fully aware that I was not a viable candidate. In the weeks following that meeting, Joy called frequently, stating that the dean was talking about when I joined the faculty in the fall. I was offered the tenure track position prior to completion of my course work, and fully recognized God's hand at work. A few weeks later, Ivan and I ventured forth on our first international trip, leading twelve American graduate students in an exploration of 100 years of British Children's Literature. What a summer!

Circuitous

GOD, THE DIRECTOR

The journey that had been orchestrated by a persistent, loving Father continued. The University of Kentucky's College of Library and Information Science offered loving mentors; one, an exacting and energetic scholar inspired me to be and do more than I ever believed possible. She coached, encouraged, and most especially applauded my teaching, scholarship, presentations, and writing. Most importantly, she "adopted" me as the daughter she had always wanted. Her closest colleague held an office across the hall from mine, and she quickly became my confidant, prayer partner and mother figure. It was an incredible cocoon of safety, support, encouragement, and love.

The God-directed tapestry I refer to as life is a winding course. Trying to harness the sequence of events illuminates the truth: the road is circuitous; we venture into the present and realize that it is often defined by the past. The writings of SQuire Rushnell in *God Winks* (2001), Rebekah Lyons' message in *You Are Free* (2017), and Richard Rohr's voice in *Falling Upward* (2011) point to the fact that our loving Fathers releases our pain from the past while building our present, and illuminating what we have learned from those chapters. It is essential that we continue to seek spiritual enlightenment as we reflect on divine intervention.

SQuire Rushnell tells us that there are no coincidences God is always at the helm. Acknowledging His presence facilitates deepening faith and growth. So, as I examine my life with the aunt, the exodus from Texas, probationary years with the guardians and marriage to Ivan, it is conspicuously clear that I was pursued, protected and directed by my heavenly Father. It was apparent that friendships were His gifts, career shifts, even when painful, were directed by divine intervention. I seldom recognized this constant presence in the moment, and frequently took years to connect the pieces.

The doctoral degree was a major God wink, and decades before learning the term. I was fully cognizant that God was on that journey, opening and shutting doors. Years later I recognized that my tenure in the Library College at the University of Kentucky was much more about Christian friendships and stability than career advancement.

An incredible mentor at the University of Kentucky was nationally acclaimed in the field of Children's Literature. The program she developed served surrounding states and held national and international recognition as an exemplar. I initially met this professional legend while presenting at a Literature Conference in the early 1980s. Just prior to my arrival at the conference, I was told that she was on-site, and my anxiety heightened. Following that presentation, I was approached with a warm introduction and congratulatory comments. Two years later I was asked to follow her as the Professor of Children's Literature. This invitation was "heady," intimidating, and unprecedented; I was completing doctoral course work when offered a tenure-track position. God was in every detail.

After signing the contract, completing the course requirements and passing the qualifying exams, Ivan and I departed the country for our first international trip. I had been invited to teach American graduate students in London for five weeks. One Hundred Years of British Literature for Children was a labor of love, and it was an idyllic summer. We were housed in King's College in Kensington, and the four day class schedule provided ample opportunity to explore England, Scotland and Wales. The faculty with whom I worked was supportive and eclectic; Ivan and I learned from students, colleagues, locals that once again, God was in the detail.

Departing the United Kingdom in late August, I had exactly two weeks before joining the Department of Library and Information Science at the University of Kentucky. The expectation was that a dissertation topic would be forthcoming as I embraced a reduced teaching load provided as an incentive to move beyond All But Dissertation (ABD) status to Dr. Cooper. I was ill prepared. It was Ivan, however, who laid the foundation for the research that would consume all free moments for the next two years.

On the flight home I was distraught that the research focus was no clearer than it had been the day we ventured to Britain. As I bemoaned my lack of preparation, Ivan reminded me of the topic that had engaged me since my initial reading of *Good Night, Mr. Tom* (Magorian, 1984). Michelle Magorian's story of the children evacuated from urban London during World War II led to questions about the depiction of that war in literature for adolescents. Again, God's direction was evident. With an excepted proposal and a lenient teaching schedule, I began the research with the assistance of two graduate students provided by the college dean. Nineteen books and much investigation led to a dissertation that was both qualitative and quantitative. Throughout this period of teaching and writing, the support from God (it was always a prayerful endeavor), Ivan and my colleagues in the Library College was unflappable. Their vigorous intellects raised the standard, while Christian love provided prayer support, and as always, Ivan was stalwart.

On November 13, 1991, the degree was bestowed, and my college celebrated. The next five years provided numerous opportunities for scholarly growth. Ivan and I returned to the United Kingdom for another summer session, I travelled to Exeter, England to learn more about international literature for children, presented at state and national conferences, hosted the Anne McConnell Conference for Children's Literature, and basked in a cocoon of professional safety.

Just when it appeared as though stability and happiness were possible my professional world disintegrated. It was the 1990s, and Information Technology was sweeping the nation. Library Colleges were closing, and books were deemed archaic. Our college became a school under the tutelage of a dean from Communications, and the literature program was decimated. Three full-time positions were allocated to one adjacent. I was devastated. Angry with God, the new dean, even the colleagues who had fully supported me, I pointed to my exemplary teaching records, scholarship, community service and evaluations, but none of it convinced the hierarchy that literature had a place in a modern library program.

During the "year of grace" given so I could secure a new position, anger consumed me. I continued to teach with passion, write and represent the college, but the blow to my ego was severe. I was deeply wounded, battered and frightened. Reluctant to acknowledge the depth of my insecurities, I was loath to trust even God. I shut myself off from colleagues, and all but Ivan. It was with trepidation that I confessed my angst to my Lord, and He, of course, demonstrated that He had a plan greater than I could imagine.

I interviewed, prayed and sought validation. Lake Erie College in Painesville, Ohio, promised the most academic freedom, and opportunities to grow. So, it was with great trepidation that Ivan and I left our beloved Kentucky home, church family, an adult son with a career in the Air Force and friends to venture to Northeast Ohio. We purchased a beautiful brick tutor on the banks of Lake Erie, and began the search for employment for Ivan. At the twenty-fourth hour he was offered the principal position in Painesville; the elementary school had housed five principals in as many years. Once again we were on God's itinerary, and could only hold on to see what He had in store. As always, He was full of surprises. One of the most significant was the friendship of our neighbor, Majel. At the time we met her, Majel was in her late eighties, an artist selling handcrafted artwork at the Cleveland Art Museum, a widow of many decades and the mother of a sixty plus adult son, living with her. Her entry into our lives was truly a gift from

God. She was an accomplished cook, gardener, host, artist and a devoted friend. The energy she embodied was contagious, and the vicarious joy she received from our adventures noteworthy. As I travelled to Britain, Ireland, China and Australia for the college, Majel followed my routes. As Ivan heralded a failing school into a sound academic program, Majel applauded. She was exactly what we needed in this new and challenging environment.

Buck's star was rising rapidly as he embraced the Air Force as an opportunity to excel, lead and serve. Our visits were too infrequent, but the family we had formed became ever closer. The loss of Buck's biological father was a time of reflection for us, as we realized the depth of belief he had in us to serve as surrogate parents. Our relationship with his father was another God-given gift, and one that freed Buck to love us as "additional" parents.

The years in northeast Ohio were liberating in many ways. Ivan soared in his role as an administrator who resurrected a school targeted to close. I expanded as a scholar and a traveler, and began to explore new academic vistas. We were healthy, stable and content, but there were missing pieces. The search for a church home did not materialize, although we looked across denominations. Our church attendance was erratic, and the much needed foundation was missing. Politics at Lake Erie College began to surface as an integral issue, and a no confidence vote for the president led us to believe that perhaps it was time to venture elsewhere. So, five years after leaving our beloved Kentucky, we were once again searching, seeking God's will.

DISCERNMENT

IT IS IN REACHING OUT THAT WE ACHIEVE. . .

So, God led us to a small Methodist college in the capitol of Delaware. Ivan resumed his teaching career, joyfully giving up administration to awaken students to the wonders of math and science. I was hired to teach Literature for Children to graduate and undergraduate students, pursue research and continue to write. It seemed like an idyllic formula.

We purchased a lovely home in a rural community, added a German Shepherd to the Scotty family, and settled into fifteen years in central Delaware. There were incredible opportunities, and many obstacles. Through all of the years, God was orchestrating.

International opportunities continued as I traveled for the college, too often without Ivan. Presenting papers, and serving as an ambassador for the college, I met amazing people, some of whom changed my life. Offering students opportunities to travel abroad was a mission for me, as I envisioned a world where we understand that as God's children we were much more alike than different.

Then in 2003, Ivan experienced the first of many signs of genetic heart disease. In the middle of the night we drove to the emergency room of the local hospital to learn that Ivan had to be transported to northern Delaware where a more experienced team of cardiologists was available. After procedures that included two stents in his valves, he had a heart attack; we later learned that it was due to the guide wire that had been left in a major vein. At this point in time (2023), he has eight stents, bi-yearly visits with the cardiologist, afib, and heart valve leakage. It has been a long journey.

It was during this venture that I began to contemplate retirement. I loved my work, and felt privileged to get paid to share the literature I loved with students, travel, write and constantly meet interesting people. In addition, I served as the Director of the International Program for years, and was able to encourage young adults to explore the world to broaden their horizons. Ivan's health issues, however, put everything into a perspective that I had not previously considered. The two absolutes in my life are my love of God and my love for Ivan. His deteriorating health, coupled with unprecedented bouts of fatigue made my vow to never retire unrealistic. The world in which I professionally lived was "heady." I was a popular professor, a well established scholar with international publications, an impressive passport and respect from colleagues. None of it mattered if Ivan was not all right.

As always, I initiated this query with prayers, prayers for Ivan's health, for guidance, for help, for answers. And as He usually does in my life, my loving Father paced His answers as I explored options.

In the fall of 2008, I was invited to present a paper in my field at the Oxford Roundtable in Oxford, England. The presentation would occur in March of 2009, and would be to an audience of forty-two scholars from around the world. I was both thrilled and terrified. As I asked God for focus, He directed not only the topic, but each step. Decades of friendship with the Scottish writer, Mollie Hunter, became the defining point. Mollie's ongoing battle with God had long been a topic of conversation as we shared international phone updates. At the age of nine, Mollie's greatly beloved father succumbed to wounds obtained in WWI, and her anger with God began. Throughout a lifetime of joy and pain, the anguish was always due to a disconnected Sovereign. So, with trepidation I asked Mollie's permission to examine her autobiographical pieces (published as fiction) for God's existence, presence, role. . .she agreed.

I commenced on a long journey of prayer, reflection, literary examination and illumination. It was a rollicking period of writing, calling Mollie, plunging back into the literature, and always asking for divine intervention. After months of labor, squeezed in between teaching and administrative responsibilities, I had an epiphany! Mollie's declaration that she was mad at God was revealed in each of the autobiographical accounts of protagonists seeking God in every venue of their lives. It was with trepidation that I made the call to Scotland to reveal what I had discovered: Mollie Hunter had been on a quest for God since the day she declared her anger with Him. Mollie listened as I outlined my discovery and solicited her permission to share it in a very public arena. The phone went "dead," and I thought that she had disconnected. After a very long silence, I heard the familiar brogue saying, "You are right, Lassie. Go ahead."

The Oxford Roundtable is daunting. Scholars from every continent convene to enlighten their peers on a tightly defined topic. The group that was identified for this auspicious task was noteworthy, and it was humbling to be a part of the company. As always, prayer kept me grounded as I reminded myself that this was to be a Psalm of Praise to the Lord who placed me in this company. Although I had presented at hundreds of conferences throughout the United States and the world, I was intimidated and fearful. The revelations took over, the audience was enthralled, and the delivery well received.

The following day I flew to Inverness, Scotland to tell a frail Mollie Hunter that she had been the "belle" of the roundtable. In typical Mollie fashion, she acknowledged that it should be so. We celebrated our friendship, her audience of appreciation in Oxford, and her admitted relationship with God. It was the last time I saw her, although we continued to talk and correspond until her death.

Two years later I was asked to return to Oxford, and again selected Mollie's work as the focal point. With her agreement, I selected historical fiction from her numerous titles to examine the protagonists' relationship with God. Many years earlier Mollie had shared a very personal vignette from her life, marriage, faith journey. . .and told me that I could share it with the world when her husband, my dear friend, Mike, was no longer alive. So, during the preparation for Oxford II, as I referred to it, I asked permission, but she was reluctant. I honored her wishes, and have put that aside for a later book. Despite the inability to include key information, the connection between this writer's spiritual journey and each of her literary ventures was emphatically established. Once again the peer group was delighted to receive new insights into the Carnagie Award winning author's faith.

Adventures, Fantasy, and Dreams in Children's Literature (McConnell-Farmer, ed., 2010) included "A Voyage of Discovery: Exploring a Kaleidoscope of Religion and Culture in the Writings of Mollie Hunter" (Cooper, S.A., 2010), and "Refocusing the Kaleidoscope" was included in *The Oxford Roundtable Journal*, 2011. The accolades were bittersweet, however. The peer group at the second Oxford Roundtable presented me with a beautiful cake and a bottle of champagne to commemorate the forty-third anniversary of my wedding to Ivan, but at the time Ivan was thousands of miles away. . .I called home tearfully, vowing never to travel without him again. It has been a sound promise.

By the time I flew home from Oxford, I was convinced that we were being directed toward retirement. Ivan's health and fatigue levels pointed to that. In addition, I was no longer open to career options that did not include Ivan. So, we began to explore options. I was invited to join the faculty at Southern Connecticut State University in their Library School, and both Ivan and I thought it might be the answer. A return to the library program would be a genuine joy, the salary was good, there were teaching opportunities for Ivan, and it met our goal to move to New England. So, I accepted, but soon had to ask to withdraw due to Ivan's failing health.

The Dean held the position open for a semester in hopes that all would stabilize and I could join them. It was not in God's plan.

We listed our lovely home, suffered through inspections and showings, and waited. Every Spring Break we boarded the train from Wilmington, Delaware to Boston, Massachusetts, then climbed on the coach from Boston to Portland, Maine. We booked bed and breakfasts, secured car rentals, and met with realtors as we looked for the retirement home God had designated. Interestingly, through four years of this routine, and ongoing prayers, we kept returning to the same small log home in western Maine. It is perched on the side of Moody Mountain with unencumbered views of North Pond and Mount Abram. The three levels face the dramatic views with walls of windows. It was in the frozen terrain of western Maine during early March that we first found it, and each year we returned as we combed the real estate listings from coast to mountains. Always it was the view declaring God's presence that was so captivating. Encapsulated by six wooded acres, remotely positioned up a dirt and gravel road, it provided the solace we were seeking. After long hours of prayer and discussion, we ultimately made an offer to purchase a log home half the size of the home we were selling.

Mountain living is different. God is here! He is in the woods, the wildlife, the mountains, the pond, the night skies. . .it is magnificent, and sometimes challenging. The fall of 2016, we resigned our teaching positions, turned the keys of the Delaware home over to the new owners, and forged up the mountain. It has been an adventure, guided by God.

JUXTAPOSITIONS

Nine months ago I observed my 75th birthday as tangible evidence of survival. In mid-March, we celebrated our 55 years of marriage. Today I am writing from a place that is deeply spiritual; God's presence is observable on our mountain. I experience Him in the woods that encapsulate our six acres, in the wildlife that meanders across the front lawn. Dramatic views of Mount Abram just beyond the glistening pond are daily reminders of His handiwork. Most poignant are the "God winks" (Rushnell, 2001), providing joyful messages of His love and intimacy.

How did I arrive at this place of safety in 2023, a year fraught with divisiveness, an international pandemic and national violence? It has been an ongoing journey for sixty-nine years, and it continues. . . The real story is how God pursues each of us, even when we are oblivious. Along the way there have been tragedies, unexpected opportunities, mentors. . .sometimes I recognize God at work in the moment, although frequently it is through prayer and reflection that His blue print becomes evident.

My intense "God time" is spent on the treadmill, usually before dawn. Most mornings as I run, I pour my heart out to our incredible Father, sharing every concern for a long list of people about whom I care intensely. I praise, cry, petition, rejoice and know that I am heard. It is a daily ritual that keeps me hopeful because I know that God is at the center, and very much in control.

BIBLIOGRAPHY

Barrie, J. M. *Peter Pan*. Oxford: Oxford University, 1991.

Burnett, Frances Hodgson. *The Secret Garden*. Boston: Godine, 1987.

Campbell, Joseph. *The Hero's Journey*. New York: HarperCollins, 1990.

Cooper, Susan A. "Refocusing the Kaleidoscope: The Protagonists Who Illuminate Mollie Hunter's Journey." In *Forum on Public Policy: A Journal of the Oxford Round Table* 1 (2011) 1–14.

———. "A Voyage of Discovery: Exploring a Kaleidoscope of Religion and Culture in the Writings of Mollie Hunter." In *Adventures, Fantasy and Dreams in Children's Literature,* edited by Judith Lynne McConnell-Farmer, 43–55. Chicago: Linton Atlantic, 2010.

Dickens, Charles. *Oliver Twist*. Ware, UK: Wordsworth Classics, 1992.

———. *A Tale of Two Cities*. London: Chapman & Hall, 1859.

Lyons, Rebekah. *You Are Free: Be Who You Already Are*. Grand Rapids: Zondervan, 2017.

Magorian, Michelle. *Good Night, Mr. Tom*. London: Kestrel, 1984.

Marshall, Catherine. *Adventures in Prayer*. New York: Ballentine, 1987.

Rohr, Richard. *Falling Upward*. San Francisco: Jossey-Bass, 2011.

Rushnell, SQuire. *God Winks*. New York: Howard, 2012.

Spyri, Johanna. *Heidi*. London: Puffin Classics, 2009.

Ten Boom, Corrie. *The Hiding Place*. Bloomington, MN: Chosen, 1971.

Wilder, Laura Ingalls. *Little House in the Big Woods*. New York: HarperCollins, 1953.

———. *On the Banks of Plum Creek*. Chicago: Harper & Row, 1953.